Shocking the Dark

Shocking the Dark

Poems by

Robert Lowes

© 2024 Robert Lowes. All rights reserved.
This material may not be reproduced in any form, published,
reprinted, recorded, performed, broadcast,
rewritten or redistributed without
the explicit permission of Robert Lowes.
All such actions are strictly prohibited by law.

Cover design: Shay Culligan
Cover art: Paul Klee, *The Goldfish*
Author photo: Saundra Lowes

ISBN: 978-1-63980-550-1

Kelsay Books
502 South 1040 East, A-119
American Fork, Utah 84003
Kelsaybooks.com

To my late parents Marvin and Hilde Lowes,
and my brother Dave

Acknowledgments

Grateful acknowledgement is made to the publications in which the following poems originally appeared, sometimes in an earlier version.

Blink: "Malpractice Attorney"
Delta Poetry Review: "I Am Comfort: A Found Poem"
The Ekphrastic Review: "The Blue Head," "Outbreak of Fear III," "Revolution of the Viaduct," "Colorful Lightning," "Dance of the Moth," "Death and Fire," "Commander in Chief of the Barbarians," "The Goldfish"
ONE ART: "Next Exit"
Passager: "It Takes a Villain"
Southern Poetry Review: "Possession," "Office Interior"
Third Wednesday: "Rapture of the Field Mouse," "Autumn Speculations," "That Stage of Life," "Étude: Prose Poem"
UCity Review: "Divine Regret," "Shagging Fly Balls," "Fine Print," "The Morning News," "A Wake," "Mention My Name for the Discount," "Sept. 1, 2019"
War, Literature & the Arts: "Such Rippling Flags"

Acorn, Akitsu Quarterly, Bottle Rockets, Chrysanthemum (Germany), *December, Failed Haiku, Frogpond, Haiku Canada Review, Kingfisher Journal, Missouri Haiku Project, Modern Haiku, ONE ART, Presence* (UK), *The Heron's Nest, The Mainichi* (Japan): Haiku

Thank You

I wish to thank a bevy of friends who also are poets. Foremost is Marjorie Stelmach, who read and responded to most of the poems in this collection. Her suggestions and encouragement were invaluable. Helpful critiques also came from Amy Debrecht, Nancy Pritchard, and Spencer Hurst, who were generous with their time. I'm particularly grateful to Ben Gaa, a writer of outstanding haiku, who revived my interest in this form. And I continue to learn about matters of taste and craft from Jason Sommer, my older brother in poetry.

I'm indebted to artists of all sorts—past and present—who inspire me not only with their work but also their lives of courage and integrity. One such person is the painter Paul Klee, whom I attempt to honor with nine poems in this collection. Most of all, I thank my wife, Saundra, for supporting me in an art that requires habits of solitude if I hope to form a relationship with readers, known and unknown.

Contents

Some Last Ditch   13

Shagging Fly Balls   15
Rapture of the Field Mouse   16
Fine Print   17
Office Interior   18
Singsong Blues   19
Dazzle   20
Divine Regret   24
Reconstructed Aryan Prayer   25
Knowledge Worker Considers Terrorism   26
Perish the Thought   27
Deep in the Defeated Country, Parsed   28
The Happy Uline Catalog   30
Preoccupations   31
Beatitudes for a Class-C Office Building   34
The Morning News   36
A Wake   37
The Temple of the Lost Cause   38

Overnight Snow: Haiku and Senryu   43

After Paul Klee: Paintings   59

Introduction   61
The Blue Head   63
Outbreak of Fear III   64
Kettledrummer   65
Death and Fire   66
Commander in Chief of the Barbarians   68
Revolution of the Viaduct   69
Dance of the Moth   70

The Goldfish   71
Colorful Lightning   72

Next Exit   73

Ex-Pentecostal   75
September 1, 2019   76
Such Rippling Flags   78
Fiftieth Class Reunion   79
The Rake in the Dumpster   81
Autumn Speculations   82
Catch of the Day   83
Packing the Swimsuits   84
The Laramide Orogeny   85
That Stage of Life   86
It Takes a Villain   87
Epitaphs of the Road   88
Next Exit   90
Mention My Name for the Discount   91
Knowledge Worker Deposes His Hand   92
Étude: Prose Poem   93
I Am Comfort: A Found Poem   94
The Devil of the Details   96
Prelude   97
Imago   98
Possession   99
Eucharistic Views   100

Some Last Ditch

Shagging Fly Balls

How many mystics
have found themselves

at the exact spot,
in center, to receive,

with upraised hand,
a heavenly body

making its descent,
and felt the hard

smack of union?
But oh, those sprints

to the right place
in the first place—

lungs burning,
heart exploding.

Rapture of the Field Mouse

He was borne aloft, half dead, in hawk talons,
and bled in hawk talons.

Soaring above the cornfield stubble,
he saw the horizon instead from hawk talons,

hill beyond hill, sky a blue pasture,
some vision for a mouse in dread of hawk talons,

which relaxed when crows mobbed the raptor.
The rodent fell to earth from reddened hawk talons

and lived to squeak again in cornfield stubble,
gazing high overhead for hawk talons.

Fine Print

I've known thin ice, loose boards,
unraveling rope,

like the trumpeting credo on
a page of scripture

with a worm of a footnote crawling
at the bottom:

"The meaning of the Hebrew
is uncertain."

Office Interior

There's no natural light in these long halls,
from the sun or moon, lightning or fireflies,
though a painting of sunset hangs on the wall.

Buried in the building, in little stalls,
workers stare at screens with straining eyes.
There's no natural light in these long halls

to mark the moods from daybreak to nightfall.
Here, the earth stops spinning. The only surprise
is a painting of sunset cock-eyed on the wall.

Tiny lights wink from every digital
gadget, a sign they're hale and energized.
There's no natural light in these long halls,

no other gifts of a window—the hoarse call
of crows, the sight of wobbling butterflies,
or a sunset painting fire on a wall.

Shadows inside are faint, if seen at all,
and faces look sick beneath fluorescent skies.
There's no natural light in these long halls,
and they've hung a sunset, hung it from the wall.

Singsong Blues

The box in the road
has lost its load.
A windowless
cardboard house

without a roof
gives drivers pause,
split second of truth.
Do they barrel through

and mash it down,
or swing around?
Upright and empty
(a spiritual mode),

the box in the road
now buckles
beneath the rubber
of a pickup truck

that doesn't swerve
or carefully curve.
Traffic that follows
fails to hallow

the flattened lump.
Thump-thump, thump-thump.

Dazzle

My god, I can't see,
driving into the late
afternoon sun, more light
than I bargained for,
a furious broken yolk
that blinds me. I nearly
clip a jaywalker,
crunch into a dump truck.
My foot hits the brake pedal,

my mind still racing.
I wait for a cooldown
to ordinary vision,
lost in the furnace
of the yellow fanatic
that puts out my eyes
like a Hammurabi judge,

the sun as dazzling
as gods used to be,
when they burned among us,
igniting bushes,
irradiating faces
of angels and prophets,
awarding tongues of fire
and night visions as bright
as a thousand flood lamps.
So says the dark ink
of sacred text

no longer scribbled.
Now we celebrate the metaphor
that god is light
at Hanukkah, Easter, Diwali.
We're content to be dazzled
on the inside, not the outside,
by a figure of speech—
words, not a flash in the flesh.

But I like the sound
of that word, dazzle—
a daddy that sizzles,
a daddy with soul,
free with a nuzzle,
since daddy is love.

As long as I don't go blind,
dazzle me, Dazzle.

Dazzle, know me to death.
Dazzle, order an extra X-ray.

Dazzle, I'm sick
of TV explainers.

Dazzle me, I want
to laugh out light.

Dazzle me a white
hot dress shirt.

Dazzle the wreck
on the road of religion.

Dazzle every Lazarus
back to breakfast.

Dazzle, love my troller.
Dazzle, love my hacker.

Dazzle scripture
into eagles.

Dazzle temples
into sandboxes.

Dazzle priests
into bubbles.

Dazzle day
into superday.

Dazzle, talk me into
my mother tongue.

Dazzle dazzle think
faster than Einstein.

Dazzle dazzle a galaxy
on each wrist.

Dazzle dazzle I see
Hank Williams, sober.

Dazzle dazzle Van Gogh
gets his ear back.

Dazzle, I'm rubbing my hands
near your dazzle,

dazzle dizzy,
drunk with dazzle.

Dazzle, should I
keep this a secret?

Dammit, Dazzle,
you're sinking
below the tree line.

Dazzle gone to drizzle
of straight-edge rays
on license plates and chrome,
the glassy corridor
of chain-store commerce,
pedestrian heads bowed down
to handy black rectangles.

How long have I been stuck
at a green light, Dazzle?

How long?

Divine Regret

> Homo homini lupus: Man is a wolf to man.

My apes have gone off course,
though their missiles can thread a window.
I didn't expect them to evolve this way,
swelling the oceans like I did once.

Their missiles assassinate through windows.
Their neutron bombs preserve Picassos.
They scum the swelling oceans with plastic.
Not so great apes—more sap than sapiens.

Their bombs are masterpieces of negation.
Why did I give them opposable thumbs?
Apes, great at decapitation, wise-guy hits.
Better that they had stayed in the trees.

So many innocents under their thumbs.
Homo homini lupus? Homo homini simia.
Better that they had stayed in the trees
than come down to pave the savannah.

The wolves are praying for my apes
to form one gigantic pack, no outcasts,
and save the last savannahs
for doleful wildebeests, dismayed lions.

Can the bipeds sign a pact for life?
I didn't expect them to evolve this way,
with nothing to teach the wildebeests and lions.
My apes are lost on the golf course.

Reconstructed Aryan Prayer

"Protect, keep safe, man and cattle."
—*The American Heritage Dictionary
of Indo-European Roots*

Protect, keep safe, man and cattle,
my walking wealth,
two and four-footed chattel.
Preserve their health.

Guard my slaves
from lameness and fever.
May the girls you gave me
always conceive.

Spare cows and bulls
from lightning and raiders.
Let udders be full
until the slaughter.

All that I've plundered,
bless in your name,
man and cattle, my herd,
raising dust on the plain.

Knowledge Worker Considers Terrorism

Walls of azaleas, red, pink, and white.
He snaps a smartphone portrait of a bee
wallowing in a blossom's pit. *Come see
our botanical garden, it's world class*, he texts out-

of-town friends, *and flush with wedding gowns*.
Bending to inspect the white asterisk
of Bethlehem's Star, breeze on his cheek, he asks
himself, *Why would our enemies want to burn down*

*or blow up this sanctuary of leaves
and petals, while toddlers skip ahead of their moms
on the limestone path? Is a suicide bomber
in the crowd?* He pauses at the Japanese

pond, its surface bumped by monstrous carp
for pellets that the people toss. *They could chop
off our infidel heads right here for their videos.*

A wrinkled Japanese couple strolls by, eyes sharp
for azaleas. *Their names end in vowels, not stops,*
he thinks, *like Hiroshima, Tokyo.*

Perish the Thought

I can't stop thinking about airborne clothes,
socks with a ticket, jetting to Boston,
masses of fabric in wrist-breaking luggage,
raptured, aloft, speeding like us.

Socks with a ticket are jetting to Boston,
slacks and skirts, enough for a week.
Raptured, aloft, on speed like us,
set to be filled, and slightly soiled.

Slacks and skirts, enough for a week,
they can always be ironed at the hotel
before they're filled on a new city's soil,
out on the town, the convention floor.

They can always be ironed at the hotel,
the wrinkled suits, the Sunday best,
for a night on the town, the expense account.
Just wait until the runway bump.

The wrinkled suits, the Sunday best
of pilgrims buckled in and chilling out,
assured they'll land, just a runway bump,
no scattered hats and coats on fire.

A chill wind buckles and bounces the pilgrims.
Masses of fabric shudder in luggage.
They've yet to scatter and ignite.
Stop me from thinking about airborne clothes.

Deep in the Defeated Country, Parsed

Deep, like a well
with no rungs on the slick stone sides.
Or deep, far into the interior,
whatever heart of darkness
lies there, vertical gloom
flipped horizontal.
As in extremely engaged
in a subject matter, say, grievance.

Or deep, meaning profound,
such as deep loss,
or lostness,
felt in a well,
in a swallowing interior,
in each subject
of the defeated country.

Defeated, as understood
by its deep Latin roots.
De, to reverse, reduce.
Facere, to make, do.
As in undo. Undo a country.

Defeated: beaten, bested,
thrashed, overpowered,
a condition of being endlessly
beaten, bested,
thrashed, overpowered.

Country, a land with borders
and laws, however breached,
and they are, in a country sullen
and forever smarting from defeat.

Country, in the general sense,
because it has forfeited its name,
no longer united, no longer
neighborly states, but encampments.

Country, a landscape,
a hinterland splinterland,
crisscrossed by asphalt,
zipping vacationers
and rumbling trucks
loaded with freezers,
king-sized beds, boots,
gasoline, Lego blocks,
and cattle seen through slots,

bodies in deep shadows, alive,
in a defeated manner of speaking,
for now.

The Happy Uline Catalog

The thick slick Bible of shipping gear

like cardboard boxes built for dishes, rifles,
bicycles, laptops, business cards.
Beautifully empty, pining for content,

they make me despair of an organized life.
Could I use some crates, export-certified?
I picture them inside intermodal containers

stacked on injection-molded plastic pallets.
Uline has the tape, the tags, the labels,
but I don't have a customer address,

much less a product. Uline, sell me a valid
destination, and goods to pack like hell.
I'll order your universal spill kit in case

you betray me, Bible of ways and means.

Preoccupations

Medical Malpractice Attorney

Harm's way has paid his mortgage off.
What doctor dares to treat his cough?

Insurance Agent

"Guard against risk" is her standard answer
and why she quit her life as a dancer.

Limousine Driver

No one can see who's first and second-class
when they sit behind the tinted glass.

Car-Dent Remover

Have tools, will travel, on a bad storm's trail.
He pulls onto a new-car lot—all hail!

Office Building Janitor

She's too tired to judge the trash she empties,
having seen it all—condoms, puke, and empties.

Radio Personality

Her voice darkens for the latest shooting news,
sparkles when she shills an Alaskan cruise.

FedEx Driver

The gross domestic product fills each box.
To her, she might as well be lifting rocks.

Retired Astronomer

One more orbit
before the obit.

Obituary Writer

Research, not grief; a morning's work on a life.
Cold calls to friends and colleagues, and last, the wife.

Dishwasher

He's found no app for scouring food off plates.
Jets of hot water scald his hands and face.

Vending Machine Restocker

Each stop on the route has stories, like Building A,
where someone gave up Cheez-Its back in May.

High-Rise Window Washer

He dangles like a spider on a thread
and meditates on last night's unmade beds.

Beatitudes for a Class-C Office Building

Blessed is the for-lease sign
tilting in the flowerbed
on rotting wooden stakes.

Blessed is the cracked flowerbed wall,
for Rome also fell.

Blessed is the elevator
that may disobey the button.

Blessed are the tenant door signs:
cast embossed bronze,
thin, wavy, stamped aluminum;
taped-up copy paper.

Blessed is the Polish handyman
who smokes and smiles,
who tends a furnace on life support.

Blessed is the therapist between sessions,
trotting to the bathroom down the hall.

Blessed is the solo attorney,
sandbagged by briefs at her desk,
for she dispenses free advice
while crossing the patchy parking lot.

Blessed is the rip
in the lobby's beige wall fabric,
a door into a Class-Z building
with magical bathrooms.

Blessed are the dead tenants
whose stenciled names
haunt parking spots.

Blessed is the insurance agent,
eighty-something, who rises
to Catskills wit in the elevator.

Blessed is the second-shift janitor
who inherited the job from his dad,
who looks you straight in the eye
without judgment.

Blessed is the dental hygienist
in blue scrubs, for she slices
the annual birthday cake
for the Polish handyman.

Blessed is the little boy
singing and bounding down the hall
to the therapist's office
ahead of his mother,

breaking the solo attorney's
chains of thought.

The Morning News

My backyard flowers committed no crimes
last night. Begonia, foxglove, sweet william—
they're innocent. Did gunshots in the dark
shake their blooms? If so, they're holding
their ground. The red and yellow columbine
hang their heads. Their roots must know
what's buried, starting with Abel and up
to the hopeless teens who spray the streets.
Maybe the columbine hear the bad news
through the rootwork from funeral wreaths
before they're clipped off and heaped
on gleaming caskets to honor the bullet-ridden.
I rub a gnarled mint leaf with my thumb
and sniff it. The scent never lasts.

A Wake

The son, husband, father, grandfather,
uncle, brother, and friend to many
holds still for eternity's camera, eyes
mashed shut by the supernova flash.
Images on a big screen automate
memory: baseball cap, wedding suit,
bass boat, oxygen tank. Other faces
flashing by match those roaming the aisles,
clustering, scattering, catching up
on retirements, stents, tomato patches,
grandkids. Little boys and girls romp
in the hall, hiding and seeking, their future
all cherries and apples. Laughter
everywhere, bleeding freely as it should.

The saddest person in the funeral home,
its director, in his cramped paneled office,
whose hangdog face suggests he's waiting
for us to leave so he won't miss his favorite
show at nine. But then, he's witnessed
generations of grief, lovefests, truces
between sisters, bodies like this one,
when they stood around other caskets.
He knows the backstories, who cheats,
and everyone knows he drinks on the job.
It's a small rural town, dying, shunned
by its high school grads and McDonalds.
Does he frown because there isn't enough
dying to stay open? I hate meeting his eyes.

The Temple of the Lost Cause

After The Christian General,
a painting by William Maughan

Long before the cranes hoisted statues
of Robert E. Lee out of public squares
to say that Black lives really matter,
I was wandering Mosby Funeral Home,
worn out by catch-up conversations
and lamentations with my cousins,
when I saw the painting of the rebel saint,
in full uniform, a snoozing white boy
in his lap, the chair plush burgundy.
Their hands held open a Holy Bible.
I knew that Lee was pious. Spotless gray,
that uniform, matching the general's full
but kempt beard and wavy combed hair.
I stood at attention, slightly stunned.

Inside the gilt frame, the Lost Cause
wasn't lost, wasn't subject to slaughter.
God's leather-bound word guarded the boy.
The artist had gifted an unreconstructed
South with a nurturing Lee, guide to youth,
and gently forgiving should they drowse
during lessons when windowpanes darken.
The chubby-cheeked pupil dreamt on,
unnudged by the general, who stared
into a middle distance, as if meeting
the eyes of the boy's unseen mother,
happy that her son was too young
to raise a musket in some last ditch
against two-to-one Union odds.

Maybe Lee was engaging a memory:
a stiff corpse or two, or thousands, lumps
in many hues of blue and gray cloth,
rising like a harvest from a field.
Or his tête-à-tête with Stonewall Jackson,
on steeds at glorious Chancellorsville
before that other Christian general took
three sixty-seven-caliber bullets
by mistake from his own doomed soldiers.
A sober icon of that last meeting hung
nearby in Mosby's mortuary, just as it did
over Southern sofas and buffets to usher
succeeding, still seceding generations
into the temple of the Lost Cause.

In the painting of Lee, Bible reader,
nary a speck of blood or mud flecked
his uniform, but bronzed cheeks and brow
recalled endless sunny days of advance,
retreat, advance, retreat, retreat,
retreat to the Petersburg trenches,
the true last ditches of the Confederacy.
I remembered a photo of that battle,
how barefoot boys sprawled dead in the dirt
next to scarecrow men, five yards apart,
the rebel lines stretched thin and thinner
by the beef-fed Army of the Potomac,
which numbered eager Black recruits
who could never have imagined Lee's lap

except to bayonet him in the balls,
this defender of home-turf Virginia,
the whole of Dixie and its slave chattel,
some ledgered with their owner's last name,
owners who might sell a little Lee's mother
to a Mississippi planter to retire a debt.
Lee's troops dubbed him the King of Spades
for commanding them to dig trench
after trench, and they took to this labor
with reverence for Marse Lee, Bobby Lee,
the Old Man, not too old to ride hard
in the saddle until Appomattox courthouse.
The Christian General's painted eyes
might have scouted battlefields post-surrender,

the lap boy now a bearded legislator,
behind a walnut desk, redeeming the South
from the black and blue of Yankee tyranny,
and restoring the righteous way, humble
and gracious, always seeking wisdom
from the Word, which in the hands of Lee
and his shut-eye student appeared to part
somewhere in the minor prophets,
perhaps where Amos says: "They sell
the innocent for silver, and the needy
for a pair of sandals . . . now I will crush you
as a cart crushes when loaded with grain."
John Brown couldn't have cursed it better.
Or else the boy had fallen asleep

in the gospels, where Christ teaches
"the first shall be last, and the last first,"
and where the damned on Judgment Day
ask Lord Least of These, "When did we see you?"
I noticed in the funeral home gallery,
carpeted for museum-hush reflection,
how the general's left hand intertwined
with the boy's as they gripped the Bible.
They'd keep the book from dropping to the floor.
But was the lad really asleep, or dead,
another casualty marbling to rigor mortis?
Here could be a fallen statue burdening Lee
as he pondered the charge, the verdict,
of Black angels and their cold steel. Yes.

Overnight Snow: Haiku and Senryu

overnight snow
reaching for the shovel
instead of the sled

company Christmas tree—
the same shiny
empty boxes

making the slush sing
speeding yellow cab
in February

cardinal on a wire
balancing
a blue sky

after white days
and gray days
pink azaleas

iris bud
sharpened
to write in purple

just as I hoped—
the pink clematis
climbing the trellis

making friends
with a guitar
then love

the nutgrass weed
I'm pulling up—I swear
it's pulling back

April breeze
yesterday's deer carcass
down to the bones

trees leafy again
I no longer see
the distant church

the morning after—
taping up torn-up
wedding photos

a therapist
seeing a therapist—
and on it goes

I stare into space . . .
a sick friend
in another city

black coffee fills
a white cup—
the night retreats

muddy river
sunburned rafter
with a Hitler tattoo

soft paddle stroke
the slow step
of an egret

river's edge—
a great blue heron's skull
and yellow coneflowers

bright green snake
too quick
to show you

endless Kansas cramped in a car

billboard lawyer
smiling
about my injury

moose on the slope
staring down
at traffic

rushing mountain creek—
can't hear myself think
so I won't

bursting
with shiny berries—
black-bear scat

empty beer pitchers our voices louder

color footage
of World War Two—
so they saw red

coming at us
for millennia now
a line of ants

sparrow's shadow
on a brick wall, flying
toward a shadow tree

alone in the exam room
examining
wires, chairs, self

moon over the city
office towers
lit for cleaning crews

bright and early
a man leaves the jailhouse
holding his shoelaces

a long ago suicide—
and still I look
twenty stories up

moonlight stroll
through the seminary grounds
jazz across the street

sparrows at my feet
the sidewalk café's
order of things

tables emptying—
the waitress
talks about her son

panhandler's sign
recycled from
an Amazon box

swarming the yard
I thought was mine
a flock of grackles

sunlit trail
a falling leaf
meets its shadow

a bench on the trail
with a plaque, a name . . .
the bluebells she saw

crisp fall air
my turn to watch others
walk to school

after the storm
walking on a sea
of yellow leaves

after the storm
a fallen tree
reveals its rot

petting a neighbor's dog
with cancer
a few seconds longer

fogged-up window
I fingertip
mountain peaks

antidepressant pill
little white moon
for the dark inside

for a second, all's well—
washed silverware
back in the drawer

December night sky
the unimaginable chill
between the stars

Christmas gift exchange—
a friend announces
he's moving away

one more New Year's Eve
the man in the moon
still gasping

frozen ground
pigeons nodding yes
to everything

the snowstorm I feared
lovely
coming down

keeping a secret
a cast-off coat
in the snow

After Paul Klee: Paintings

Introduction

Paul Klee (1879–1940) was a Swiss-born German painter who was hard to classify in terms of style. He might have considered that ambiguity a compliment. Many museumgoers probably are familiar with the whimsical, childlike, and color-coded work from his early and middle years. The full range of his paintings tells a lesser-known story. A teacher in the legendary Bauhaus art school, Klee ran afoul of the Nazi regime and its wretched Aryan aesthetics in the 1930s. The Nazis shut down the Bauhaus, fired Klee from a university professorship, and exhibited his work in their notorious Degenerate Art exhibit of 1937—a badge of honor but also an indication of his pariah status. During that same period, Klee battled a painful autoimmune disease called scleroderma that hardened his skin and damaged vital organs. The condition eventually led to his death in 1940 in Switzerland, his safe haven from the Nazis.

Undaunted by his own body and the body politic, Klee painted with crippled hands to the very end of his life, taking an artistic stand against fascism along the way. His late-life canvases, often dark and runic, prophesied both the Holocaust and his own death. Yet they hinted at a better world elsewhere. Whether he was a cubist, a surrealist, an expressionist, or a combination of all three camps makes no difference. What matters is that he was a mensch and a much-needed example in our time.

The Blue Head

How fortunate you are, to call
the sky your mother,
though you must inhale
more than its blue comfort.

There's no denying
tornado green and blizzard white.
Your button eyes
smuggle in midnight

while your tiny lips press together,
deprived of words
for the fickle weather,
the hours dealt like playing cards.

Outbreak of Fear III

We have done the work of the enemy
by imagining ourselves dismembered:

the severed head crying for the severed leg,
the arms sawed up for the fireplace.

Our actual fate may not be as horrendous,
but we have already fled our flesh

in anticipation. The blood is drained out,
rendering skin the color of ash.

Kettledrummer

In the year of your death,
degenerating, but not degenerate,
as the Nazis had brayed,

you dared to paint him,
his drumsticks pounding
like an aroused heart,

pounding out the order
to abandon your hardening body.
You marched as commanded,

you who once wandered
the most idle line.
You fleshed the drummer

with a few strokes of tar.
For relief, two smears
of dried blood.

His hideous lone eye,
once fixed on you,
is fixed on me

until I twist away
toward the next canvas
in a careless heartbeat.

Death and Fire

> "I cannot be understood in purely earthly terms.
> For I can live as happily with the dead
> as with the unborn."
> —Excerpt from Paul Klee's epitaph

Was this another epitaph?
What were you saying
when you painted TOD,
your native word for death,
on the face of a man
smiling crookedly in fire,

more a skull than face,
more an oven's serene
red-yellow glow
than woodpile blaze,

as if you had crematoriums
on your mind in nineteen forty,
the year you died,
just as your persecutors,
who branded you degenerate,
had turned industrialists,
burning entire peoples.

Perhaps you were imagining
Nebuchadnezzar's furnace,
where three faithful men didn't die.

Weren't you burning inside
walls of hardening skin,
finesse deserting
your stiffened fingers?

Your brush managed
rough black lines,
perfect charrings
for the characters of death,
which you painted twice,

once on the ashen mask,
its very eyes and mouth
spelling TOD, and again
with the man's upraised
arm and right-angle palm,
a golden orb on top,
like a nimbus
waiting for its saint,
the lopsided face itself
forming the final letter.

Words live on in the fire.
The smile, however
mangled, persists.
And above, in the corner,
a stick figure strolls
into the colorful heat,
as if of its own free will.

You might be saying welcome.
Then paint me in.

Commander in Chief of the Barbarians

What will you do, steely man,
after your warriors parade
their stained flags
through the smoking city?

Your straight lines
admit to nothing soft,
but orphans wail, and someone
must lay down his sword

to learn the local tongue,
the strange machines,
new ways of stacking
stone into walls and towers.

And when you're too old
to ride all day, will you
pension here? Will your daughters
mince native dances

while you drowse by a fireplace
and its clever, glowing
brickwork, oblivious to the next
shudder of hoofbeats?

Revolution of the Viaduct

The arches were ordered to line up
and stand still for inspection.

But look, they have broken ranks,
and the secret blood of stones

has risen to the surface—
yellow, orange, pink.

The arches are walking our way,
one stiff leg in front of the other.

If we are liberators,
they will carry us on their shoulders.

If we are slave masters,
watch out for their feet.

Dance of the Moth

A shaft of light impales you.
Over and over, you throw yourself on it.
What good is faith if I pray

just on my good days, or bad days?
I crave your constant, reckless spirit.
A shaft of light impales you

like a bright Roman nail. You fly
upward to take the hit.
What good is faith if I pray

like a moper to get my way
while you get used up, to the last bit?
A shaft of light impales you,

but not as specimen pinned in a tray.
You're lively as light, on the good foot
of good faith. So I pray

to say my prayers the way
the Irish fling or the hip hop it.
A shaft of light impales you
good. You're faith's glad prey.

The Goldfish

The center burns with a fish of gold.
Blue-green murk wets its flesh of gold.

A body electric, Whitman's pet,
shocks the dark with a flash of gold.

Muted juniors swish to the edges,
fleeing a light so flush with gold.

If I touch it, will I shine too,
like a son of fish, refreshed by gold?

Colorful Lightning

An artist is drawing tonight
with golden chalk.

It's nothing that makes sense,
nothing that would answer prayer,

just jagged brilliant lines.
He loves these lines,

but loves even more the act
of the wandering, downward stroke.

No sooner is he finished
than he wipes the blackboard clean

so his free hand
can crack the darkness again.

Next Exit

Ex-Pentecostal

I no longer treasure the old cult

of certitude, the woolly hymns,
the prophet's answer,
the laying on of hands,

trust in divine whims,
dismay at cancer,
blind heroic stands

against tectonics of history,
that backwater feeling
while rivers run to the sea.

But I remember the mystery
of weightless prayer, the healing
of wounds unknown to me,

occult as in hidden, like tumors and treasures.

September 1, 2019

Dust of panzer columns
stabbing Poland
eighty years ago today.
Stuka dive-bombers,
like falcons over Warsaw.

My Munich mother,
twelve years old then,
perhaps posing pretty
for her father's Leica
near the swoosh and spray
of Sendlinger Tor fountain,
four years from rubble.
Loudspeakers above
the cobblestones blared,
"The Jews are our misfortune."

My father, four lean years
before boot camp. Maybe
baling hay with his brothers
in the droning, chirping
fields of Southeast Missouri.
Race was a chuckle
at suppertime, a warning
to the darkies to stay
outside the stadium fence.
He came from German stock.

From that day on in 1939,
history maneuvered
my parents like chess pieces
until they occupied
adjacent squares in Munich.

They wrote a treaty
to run their fingers
through each other's hair.
They were both born
with a good head of hair,
their gift to me,
and the only thing I want
to hear about bloodlines.

Such Rippling Flags

As a kid, I once saw old man Starsinger,
a veteran of the War to End All Wars,
doze off in his easy chair. He had been gassed
but survived to strong-arm a drill press.

Now my father's D-Day brothers retreat
in ambulances and hearses. Men once straight
as their rifles teeter as they stand for applause
at Veterans Day concerts, their white shocks

of hair like cotton bolls on spindly stems. Men
I could topple with a nudge chased Nazis
across France, tossed chocolate to orphans.
Every year fewer of them rise from the seats.

In their tracks are grunts whose frozen fingers
squeezed triggers in Korea, and after them,
the class of 'Nam, which rocked to "Purple Haze"
like I did, a few safe years behind.

Too many boys love explosions on screens.
They answer back with raspy roars. What should
I tell them about the march that begins
with bugle calls and such rippling flags

and ends with a wheelchair's hiss? I've outlived
the man who waded onto Omaha Beach
glinting at me from an Army photo, without
a wrinkle, hat cocked, still mum about it all.

Fiftieth Class Reunion

on the parking lot
I think I spot . . .
he's a little stooped

in the doorway
recognizing
old playmates

I age backwards
Robert Bob
Bobby

signing the nametag
no retracing
shaky letters

shouts laughter
conversation static
no teacher shushing

milling about
averted glances
sudden grins

taut skin
of surgery
around her eyes

yearbook photos
of the deceased
looking better than us

heart repairs
make me and her
brother and sister

stage-four survivor
the reflex of my hand
clutching his shoulder

buffet line
we've never left
the cafeteria

life stories
in two minutes
then, our gardens

basketball star
out to pasture
on the golf course

searching the eyes
of the chipper
white supremacist

can't help
looking across the room
at an old crush

scrunching together
for the class photo
my face in a gap

leaving the hive
waving
to a few

back on the parking lot
I relive
the unexpected hug

The Rake in the Dumpster

So many falls, so many leaves—you served
me well, prodding castoffs from maple trees
to the street where kids could leap into soft heaps.
But now you're missing teeth and paint; the curve
of time has come for you, as it will for me.
Thanks for what you gathered. Now go to sleep.

Autumn Speculations

Leaves twirl down to the grass
and I scan the obit page

over scrambled eggs and coffee.
The mounting curiosity—

who has crossed over?
They're indisputable pioneers,

these motionless bodies
who perhaps in some new physics

now trek at outrageous speed
past our outermost galaxies

to a lush black pasture
where they float and flash

like fireflies, and just beyond them,
the angels I've read about.

Catch of the Day

Sleek gliders, not plodders like my kind.
We were born divorced. I can't breathe down there.
They can't breathe up here. I enter their world
by ruse and proxy (lurid lure, impaled minnow)
and only to plunder it (long-jawed northern,
frowning bass). My rod twitches like knocks
on the door, and I reel one up into the sun

where I praise the jewel-like greens and blues
of shingled scales, treasure no longer obscured
by water. It's a brutal way to love,
when they come to you as conquests, not gifts.
Yet fish inflict a final revenge. As my teeth
grind up the snow-white flesh at dinner,
the slenderest bone nicks the roof of my mouth.

Packing the Swimsuits

For Kay Drey

She summered in the Great North Woods.
Her children listened for the loons.
She swam Hen Lake to prove she could.

She didn't want to spoil her brood
with cable TV in hotel rooms.
She summered in the Great North Woods

where the cabin chairs were scratched and chewed.
They ate their soup with thrift-shop spoons
and swam Hen Lake to prove they could.

They honored where the birches stood.
Their pocketknives brought none to ruin
those summers in the Great North Woods.

The kids outgrew that latitude.
She and her husband sailed alone
on the Whitefish Chain as best they could.

The moonstruck waters understood
why she listened for the laughing loon.
She summered in the Great North Woods
and swam Hen Lake to prove she could.

The Laramide Orogeny

Gazing on a long, jagged smile of stone,
I query Google: What formed the Rockies?

Reply: the Laramide orogeny, the range's
labor pains millions of years ago.

What a lilt, what a lightness, that Laramide
orogeny. I hear a pony neighing. I sniff

the air, suddenly as young as the rocks are old.
Oh my Laura, oh my Jenny. May I always

celebrate my own orogeny, rise up
to Orion, bare my peaks to the sun,

wear a snowcap come winter.
Who needs cocaine, three cups of joe,

when I can feel orogeny's tickle,
and who needs granite slabs, the creeks

they sweat? The word itself suffices,
sweeping down on me like a piney wind.

That Stage of Life

"I don't want to," the toddler says.
His "no" is atomic and blubbery.
He goes limp when you try to lift him,
a heavy sack of refusing.

Don't want to eat or nap or bathe.
Don't want my soggy diaper changed.
He is the most oppressed of humans,
his eyes damp with accusing.

Father of insurrection and strife,
he declares himself lawless and free,
yet appeals to any court he can find,
a nana, some benefactor.

Bend to his will, his urgent whim,
hand over the withheld cookie or toy,
and his pout quickens to the grin
of a consummate actor.

It Takes a Villain

to make the cars, and drive the cars,
and drill for oil, and ship oil,
and refine oil, and deliver gas
to filling stations to fuel the cars,

and raise the cows, and slaughter cows,
and butcher cows, and fry ground beef
for the mother in the McDonald's
drive-through, idling out exhaust

and checking for texts from her parents
on a smartphone plugged overnight
into a kitchen outlet, a node
of an electrical grid, powered

by coal someone plundered
from a Kentucky hilltop stripped of trees
that once removed their share
of carbon dioxide from the sky,

that blue scroll written over
with clouds of acid rain
and contrails from jumbo jets,
like the one bearing grandparents

to visit a two-year-old boy
burbling in the back seat of the car
in the McDonald's drive-through,
headed to the airport

for a joyous reunion
on a day of record-setting heat,
and plans to get wet and wild
on a vanishing beach.

Epitaphs of the Road

Frontal Crash

The red-light runners filled me with dread.
I looked left and right, but not ahead.

Rear-Ended

I braked in the work zone to avoid a fine.
The trucker in the mirror—he turned out fine.

Drunk Driver

I didn't have my wits, only my nerve,
when I gunned it to eighty on the downhill curve.

Nodding Off

I tried to drive straight from Cleveland to Denver.
Then I dreamed I did. Then I woke up forever.

So Pedestrian

I had the walk sign, I was in the right—
an argument I lost with the cab that night.

Motorcyclist, No Helmet

I was loving the feel of wind in my hair
when I launched headfirst into the air.

Car Bomb

Old gangsters with rivals shouldn't relax.
I checked just the tires on my Cadillac.

Suicide by Train

I drove to the tracks and parked my pickup truck.
The life insurance paid—at last, some luck.

Carjacked

I lost my ride. The next two rides were worse.
First the ambulance. Then the hearse.

Deer

It crashed through the windshield out in the sticks.
I was one with nature as our bloodstreams mixed.

Next Exit

Should I regret my hours on the highway,
the manic weaving of high-speed sheet metal
to shop for walking shoes, disrobe for doctors?
Pigeons swirl above the cloverleaf.
A dog carcass stains the asphalt shoulder.
Bumper stickers proclaim schools of thought.

I'm thinking thoughts, slower than the traffic.
They're shaped like wheels, nickels, pond ripples,
orbits, the wedding bands of Saturn. Each thought
hides a nucleus, a sweet spot, a seed.
A straight shot to the center pleases me
more than endlessly surfing circumferences.

My white-line fever breaks at thirteen miles.
If I saw flashing lights, I can't recall.

Mention My Name for the Discount

Our main AM station sounds faraway,
the voices of the drive-time hosts
cloudy and makeshift, like a bad
recording of a bad recording.

They're talking about panhandlers
who work the highway entrances,
the sadness of it all, and the fear
they may carjack instead of beg.

My ears are pricked when one host
breaks off to shill for a company
that builds patios, her spiel
chatty and confidential, as if she's

a hitchhiker in the passenger seat
who's sharing affordable bliss.
The radio keeps coughing up static,
and I want to cough it up too.

Knowledge Worker Deposes His Hand

Can a hand that grasps an iPhone grip
ideas? Do ideas feel like stone or wood?
Maybe I should count off ten like Moses did.
But opposable thumb, why so flip?

Ring finger, do you have a special touch
for my wife? Fingerprints, confess.
Thumb, are you pro antithesis?
Fingernails, you can't deny an itch.

Where's the virtue, wrist, in your subtle twist?
Tell me, knuckles, what it means to hate.
If I bury my head in my hands, has light
left the room? Fingers, should I drum you fast,

and will you always outnumber me
and cast the final vote and point the way?

Étude: Prose Poem

A prose poem fizzes like a burning fuse and ends with a faint pop. It doesn't want to slap people in the face with beauty. It's suspicious of light and night and right. It trains a feral gaze at ballroom dancers.

It wears a pair of jeans every day of the year—gray, black, but mostly blue. If a prose poem doesn't get published, it's hospitalized and medicated. Where the psychiatrists wear jeans. It's a very small world.

I Am Comfort: A Found Poem

> Text from electric fan ads,
> 1900 through 1960

Superior to those breeze makers
in the hands of slaves.

Arctic Aire. Kwik Kool.
Jack Frost. Polar Cub.

Ready to search out
stagnant air. Lazy air. Bad air.

What a blessing Polar Cub is.
How grateful you are.

Lively air. Fountains of air.
Ocean breeze ahoy!

Don't suffer this summer
as you did last.

The celebrities on this page
have the right idea.

Air-Jet Riviera. Sea Gull.
Imperial Silver Swan.

Bewitching. Smart as a Paris gown.
Its soft satin finish.

What cultured women
have long wanted.

She dresses in coolest comfort.
More and better work.

All the long sultry afternoon
when your friends are away at the lakes.

Phone for a fan.
Why swelter longer?

I stand between millions
and the blazing sun.

The Devil of the Details

> "The color of the tickets upsets me."
> —Franz Kafka

A blue ticket, but too pale,
as if stinting on dye,

and oily stains
on the canvas big top,

the red-nosed clown
emerging from the porta potty,

the merry-go-round operator,
his missing front tooth.

Too much ice in the Coke.
Too little shade.

Horse manure on his new shoes.
Chubby acrobats.

Not what he imagined
when he was ten.

And the laughter—
the laughter upsets him.

Prelude

A straggle of musicians took the stage
in scattered chairs for a random symphony,
doodled, disconnected notes, on edge,
the will to perfect, their only harmony.

A cellist coaxed his fingers to limber up.
A flautist flew a solo one more time.
A trumpeter exercised her cold, tight lips.
The kettle drummer tuned the rum-tum-tum.

Unable to decipher the nameless din,
I would have deserted my seat in the audience
if the full orchestra hadn't pitched in
to drone an A, and then play me into a trance

with *Scheherazade,* the jumbled, practiced parts
now a breathing life, a beating heart.

Imago

Monarch, you shame the tight,
petite milkweed blossoms,
red and yellow,
with the unfurled robe
of your dusty orange wings,
veined with black
like the stained glass
in the temple of lovemaking.

And the white polka dots
on your black body
and wing trim—that's oomph.
They make me forget
your plump, clownish
caterpillar days,
your baggy chrysalis days.

Such a slender tube
you lower to the milkweed's
intimate parts for nectar,
taking without harming,
like the rabbit cropping grass
that keeps greening.
Your wings open and close
in slow motion applause
for your own satiety

as you sway
on a windblown bed
of stem and petals.

Possession

> "When they came to Jesus, they saw the man who had been possessed by the legion of demons, sitting there, dressed and in his right mind; and they were afraid."
> —*Mark 5:15*

They inch up to me quietly these days
and I can read the fear in their hard gazes.
They half expect me to erupt in a blaze

of old madness, slashing my wrists to lick
the bloody rivulets, cracking sticks
across my head, eating worms until I'm sick.

And then I shock them even more: "He prays
as if someone's listening. He squanders his days
thanking God for birds." They brand my ways

baffling and hurry back to baking bricks,
threshing wheat and barley, trimming their wicks.
They liked me better as a lunatic.

I'm still an outcast, alone in my praise.
Last night I carved a cypress crucifix.

Eucharistic Views

I kneel. Priests loom over me.

By now they know the crease-map of my palms,
the pink blank faces of my thumbnails,
what hairs on my head won't lie flat.

They see arthritic fingers up and down
the altar rail, warts, where rings once circled,
shiny scalps, true hair color at the roots.

When my devotion weakens, I peek
at shoes below the priestly gowns: scuffed,
polished, modest, modestly vain.

No one will be perfect after we eat
the wafers dipped in pinot noir, just rough
drafts until they bury you and me, when

we're laid down and priests loom over us.

About the Author

Robert Lowes is a former journalist whose first collection of poetry, *An Honest Hunger* (Resource Publications, an imprint of Wipf and Stock Publishers), came out in 2020. His poems have appeared in journals such as *The New Republic, December, The Christian Century, Modern Haiku, Southern Poetry Review, Big Muddy,* and *The Journal of the American Medical Association.* For eight years, he was a reporter for *Medscape Medical News,* an online publication for clinicians operated by WebMD. There he wrote about a plethora of subjects: the Affordable Care Act and its journey to the Supreme Court, infectious diseases, drug recalls, Medicare fraud, electronic health records, and the opioid crisis, to name a few. As a freelance journalist, he investigated white-supremacist groups and explored the lives of career waiters and bartenders. Seven years ago, he took up the guitar. He lives with his wife Saundra in suburban St. Louis, MO.

For more information, visit:
robertlowes.com